# EXPERIENCE DESIGN FOR CUSTOMER SERVICE

# EXPERIENCE DESIGN FOR CUSTOMER SERVICE

## *HOW TO GO FROM MEDIOCRE TO GREAT!*

Mark W. Stanley

JONES MEDIA
PUBLISHING

Jones Media Publishing
10645 N. Tatum Blvd. Ste. 200-166
Phoenix, AZ 85028
www.JonesMediaPublishing.com

Disclaimer:

The author strives to be as accurate and complete as possible in the creation of this book, notwithstanding the fact that the author does not warrant or represent at any time that the contents within are accurate due to the rapidly changing nature of the Internet.

While all attempts have been made to verify information provided in this publication, the Author and Publisher assume no responsibility and are not liable for errors, omissions, or contrary interpretation of the subject matter herein. The Author and Publisher hereby disclaim any liability, loss or damage incurred as a result of the application and utilization, whether directly or indirectly, of any information, suggestion, advice, or procedure in this book. Any perceived slights of specific persons, peoples, or organizations are unintentional.

In practical advice books, like anything else in life, there are no guarantees of income made. Readers are cautioned to rely on their own judgment about their individual circumstances to act accordingly. Readers are responsible for their own actions, choices, and results. This book is not intended for use as a source of legal, business, accounting or financial advice. All readers are advised to seek services of competent professionals in legal, business, accounting, and finance field.

Printed in the United States of America

ISBN-13: 978-1-945849-77-0 paperback
JMP2019.1

# DEDICATION

This book is dedicated to all those who practice, and influence, #ExperienceDesign.

# CONTENTS

# Author's Preface

*"In wisdom gathered over time I have found that every experience is
a form of exploration."*

**-Ansel Adams**

I HAD THE good fortune to attend the College of Extraordinary Experiences, a designed-experience journey that aims to equip participants with the mindset, insight, and network to step into the experience economy and design something truly extraordinary. This event takes place at Czocha Castle in Poland, which dates back to the thirteenth century. Down in the bowels of a castle this old, one can find many interesting things, including several dungeons.

The first evening we were invited down to one of the dungeons, which had been set up as a bar, to have a drink. There were two guys tending bar and taking drink orders. When it was my turn, the bartender known as "Alex" asked me what I wanted to drink. I don't normally order drinks in a bar, and didn't really have a specific drink in mind, so I said, "surprise me!" He asked me which alcohol to start with, and I offered up "vodka." With that, he turned around and went to work.

A few minutes later, he produced a drink. It didn't look like anything I'd ever seen before, didn't smell like anything I'd expect in a bar, and as it turns out, didn't taste like anything I'd ever had before. Whatever it was, it was amazing. I took one sip and smiled. He smiled back, knowing he'd just created a moment.

The next night we all made our way back to the dungeon bar in the castle. When we walked in, the two bartenders from the night before were there and asked the crowd what they would like to drink. The "other" bartender looked at me and said, "You first!" But when he did, Alex took over, looked at me with a smile, and said, "I've got this!" He then produced exactly the same thing he'd made for me the night before. And again, he delivered the drink, observed my reaction, and smiled.

What Alex did was extraordinary in many ways. He figured out what I wanted, he delivered it, and he created a positive memory that has stayed with me ever since. I'm pretty sure he did this every night for many of his customers, but that doesn't really matter. What he does for other customers is between them. What matters is what he did for me to make my experience different, unique—*personal*. No one else got the same drink; this one was mine!

Here's the interesting part: somehow, he made it seem easy, as if this were the most normal thing in the world. *But it wasn't.* It took skill, planning, and determination on his part to make it happen. This was theater at its finest, with a stage, props, and a talented actor who figured out how to draw the audience into the performance and create something magical.

That's what this book is all about: creating memorable service experiences.

This book is *not* a deep dive into experience design. It is meant to provide a framework of principles, ideas, methods, and techniques that will influence your thinking as you work through the development of *your* plan. As Joe Pine says, "SERVICES are time well saved; EXPERIENCES are time well spent."

One more thing. I'm not telling you it's going to be easy; I'm telling you it's going to be *worth it*.

And for the record, events in this book are all drawn from actual experiences, but some of the names have been changed to protect the innocent.

# ACKNOWLEDGEMENTS

To my parents, Frank and Marilou, for teaching me how to
think and to walk like I have someplace to go.
To my partner, Vince, for keeping me sane.
To my cousin Maureen, my lifelong friend Cynthia, and CoEE
alumna Marina Terteryan for making me write this book.
To Paul, for fostering an environment that encourages people
to explore the art of the possible.
And to Wanda, who always makes me smile.

# INTRODUCTION

*"My job is not to make up anybody's mind but to make the agony of decision making so intense that you can escape only by thinking."*

**-Fred Friendly**

As A CONSUMER, think about your experience dealing with iconic companies. Disney. Apple. Amazon. Zappos. Starbucks. IKEA. Coca-Cola. Lego. Every single one of them brings an instant connection to memories: most often pleasant, but always emotional. That's not an accident. It's the result of highly focused thinking about experience design to create memories tied to these brands. It's what separates the ordinary from the isolated few that consumers will choose to visit time and again. Funnily enough, it's less about the product or service, and more about how it makes you feel. With all the variables that go into the recipe, how do the lucky ones manage to sort it all out? One thing seems clear: it starts with curiosity. I have it. And I'm betting you do too.

I've been practicing some form of customer service most of my life. At the age of nine, I took on a job delivering newspapers six afternoons a week. Schoolwork and playing with friends had to wait; customers wanted their paper. Moreover, I learned a very important lesson: they wanted their paper only and exactly the way they wanted it. Some liked it in the metal tube attached to the post below the mailbox. Some wanted it under the mat. Some liked it inside the storm door. At the same time, every single day. Clean and dry. No exceptions. And if there was any deviation, several of my customers let me know when I came at the end of the month to collect their payment. One woman paid me in quarters, sharing every service failure she felt she'd incurred with each and every quarter delivered. Even at the age of nine, I was smart enough to figure out that it was easier to deliver the paper only and exactly as she liked it than to endure her wrath for failure, quarter by quarter.

In the ensuing years I held many positions related to service. I worked my way through college at a car dealer as a clerk in the parts department and later on as a service writer. I discovered that there were some people who had years of experience and simply needed some assistance. I also discovered that most people were completely flummoxed by anything related to automobiles and knew they were at our mercy. They were placing an incredible amount of trust in us to do the right thing, get them on their way, and not charge an arm and a leg to do it.

For over twenty years I worked in the airline industry, which is probably the single largest source of material for stand-up comedians. I became intimately familiar with the reality that there are some things you can control and some you cannot. The customer will often blur the lines between the two, largely through no fault of their own. How many times have you made it to the airport on time only to discover the word *delayed* on the monitor for your flight? If I happened to be the first agent that customer encountered, they rightly wanted to know why the flight was delayed, when the flight might leave, how it would affect their connection, and whether they would make it to their destination on time. The customer didn't care about *what* caused the delay.

I eventually transitioned to contact centers, where I worked in every position there. I've answered phones, configured equipment, massaged work schedules, and managed the entire operation. I've been part of mergers and acquisitions and built and grown centers. As a consultant, I've helped many customers in a wide variety of industries do the same. Along the way, I've witnessed just about everything on the spectrum, from face-palm failures to over-the-top joy. Some of it was handled pretty well; much of it was a learning experience. It all depends on your perspective.

In the end, customer service really comes down to blind faith in humanity. Sooner or later we all run up against a problem we can't solve on our own, and we rely on the kindness of strangers to help us out. Done well, the results stay with us for a lifetime. The question is, what are the ingredients that cause that to happen? What are the drivers behind memorable service experiences?

At some point, all of the knowledge I've gained over the years has become seasoned, refined, and curated to the point where it's worth sharing. That's why this book exists. I have a keen awareness of what customers really want, the frustrations that front-line service staff have when they're caught between a customer and their manager or company policies, the bean counters who only want things done at the lowest possible cost, and the personal challenge each of us has in delivering an experience that stands apart. This is not a philosophical ideal; the concepts presented here are tried and true, block-and-tackle ideas that can be implemented and will produce results.

Along the way, I've found that nearly every company will likely wrestle with at least one of three things:

1. How can we deliver service that others look up to and envy?
2. We have a limited budget and limited authority, and we work in a matrixed organization where no one single person can make a decision.
3. The company hasn't felt enough pain to believe change is necessary.

With that in mind, I've assembled some concepts that are designed to help you create a vision your company can embrace; break away from the pack and develop a reputation for industry-leading service; and control costs and find new sources of revenue. Even if you've got the basis of a plan and have leaders who are attempting this kind of change, these concepts will help you bring it down from thirty-nine thousand feet to ground level without losing the big picture.

Apart from the publicly stated excuses that keep companies from embracing change, I would be remiss if I failed to mention what I have often found to be the *real* impediments.

- This is bigger than me. It might fail, the company could be in trouble, my department will get the blame for this if things go wrong, and people could lose their jobs. More importantly, I am at personal risk if I rock the boat, I will be exposed as a fraud, and I fear that I am going to lose my job if I speak up.
- There are blockers in the company who will keep me from achieving the goals because they don't like change, they placed their bet on a different approach that hasn't worked and are

now at risk of being exposed, or they simply lack the vision to see what needs to be done.

- These ideas are too big for us; we're a very conservative company. We tried some of these things in 1973 and they didn't work. There might be "unknown unknowns" that nobody thought of. What you are recommending will cost too much money.

The reality is this: everything I propose here can be done at most companies in less than a year, the cost will be minimal, and you probably already have the right people in place to do it. I know this to be true because I've seen it happen time and again. And every time I've been involved in these initiatives, I've discovered common ground. To be sure, EVERY company that succeeds had the same misgivings. The difference is that THEY took a chance.

You cannot know everything, and there will never be a perfect time to take action. What you can do is know 80 percent of something, build a team of smart people, and operate in a nimble way to adjust on the fly as you learn more.

I have written this book as a guide for anyone who owns the responsibility of serving customers and is in a position to change the way things are done. That might be a team leader, a supervisor, a manager, a vice president, or the chief customer officer. If you are curious, like to challenge the status quo, and need some inspiration, you've come to the right place.

So, here's what this book will do for you:

1. Help you figure out what customers really need from you (known as the **jobs to be done**) and how good you are now at understanding what the customer is asking for. (WHAT)

2. Help you figure out how to do the job efficiently and how that compares to the way you're doing things today. There are three players: the consumer, the employee, and the company. All three want something out of the deal. How can you find the right balance to satisfy all three participants? (HOW)

3. Help you understand why it's important to make the job effective by creating a memorable experience, and what kind of experience you're currently delivering. (WHY)

4. Help you talk about the new concept within your organization and gain collective ownership, make it adaptable, and make it resilient. (WHO, WHERE and WHEN)

5. Provide examples to see how this works in action.

This combination of principles, tools, and techniques is really meant to get your creative juices flowing. How you actually solve for this within your organization will be unique to your set of needs and the limits imposed on you by others. But at least you will be armed with the information you need to ask the right questions, make people uncomfortable with the status quo, and open their minds to ideas on how things could be with a little effort.

No company that aimed for mediocre ever survived. Disney, Apple, Amazon, Zappos, Starbucks, IKEA, Coca-Cola, Lego. Not one of those companies has ever been called mediocre. They have brands that speak in a very loud voice and make it clear: we're really, really good at what we do because we're really, really focused on how we're going to make you feel.

Do you want that as well? If so, you have to dream big, have realistic plans, and fuel them with passion.

# CHAPTER 1:
# EXPERIENCE DESIGN IN
# CUSTOMER SERVICE

*"Ninety percent of adults spend half their waking lives doing things*
*they would rather not be doing at places they would rather not be."*

**-Barry Schwartz**

CUSTOMER CONTACT CENTERS have been around for half a century. In those five decades we've witnessed the introduction of amazing levels of technology and automation spanning the range from toll-free numbers to artificial intelligence. Most of the innovations have centered around efficiency measures designed to control the cost of service delivery. For example, interactive voice-response systems were meant to replace low-level, redundant agent tasks with automation. These allowed callers to use "the machine" to do things like obtain account balances, process payments, and discover what movies would be playing at the nearest theater.

Along the way, we've managed to squeeze every last ounce out of the traditional notion of "customer service," and we've practically eliminated the "customer" in the process. We've done everything we can with self-service and scripted agents, and we've outsourced every last thing imaginable. What we haven't done is make the service experience any better (or memorable) for the consumer or for the people involved in the service-delivery process.

## VARIABLES

To be fair, many companies have adopted language in their mission statement that seeks to pay tribute to their valued customers—language that suggests they are "customer-centric" in everything they do. The problem with this is that it's the wrong approach. It's largely empty rhetoric, it's not measurable, and it speaks to means, not ends. But what if we started at the end and worked backward? What if we got curious about the customer? What if we hired people that have brains, equipped service staff with the training and tools they need to do their job in a professional way, and then ... let them do their job? What if we embraced a process that made service fulfilling for everyone involved?

Truly memorable experiences find the right balance between problems and solutions. In the fourth century BC, Aristotle shared his rhetorical appeals in the form of a triangle consisting of logos, ethos, and pathos. We can apply that same model to the way companies interact with their customers, asking:

- Logos (Logic): Is your service-delivery process logical? Does it make sense to the average customer and employee?
- Ethos (Credibility): Is your company credible? Do customers and employees trust you to do the right thing?

- Pathos (Emotion): Do you understand the emotional connection people have with you? Are you telling a story that resonates with the audience?

Some companies excel in one of these areas. Some excel in two. Few excel in all three. It's not that they don't want to; they just never found the time to work out how to do it. They wish they had more time and hope for a day when they will. But it turns out that wishing and hoping is not a strategy for success. Nor is the approach that favors "low-hanging fruit." Anyone can pick low-hanging fruit; the good stuff is on top!

We know there are some parts of the service-delivery process that may be unpleasant but are unavoidable. For example, certain industries are regulated and require agents to read disclosures verbatim to customers. Sometimes the contact center is "experiencing higher than normal call volume, and all agents are speaking with other customers," such as when severe weather strikes. There isn't an awful lot that can be done about that; it's just life. But there are other parts of the service experience that are controllable and that can—and should—be addressed.

In *PIG Strategy: Make Customer Centricity Obsolete and Start a Resource Revolution*, Sampson Lee illustrates the connection of emotions to the service experience and explains the importance of branded pleasures and "good" pains. He depicts the customer journey over time and shows the emotional state of the customer at each step in the journey. This makes it possible to know whether or not the pleasure or pain experienced supports the brand. It also quantifies the experience by showing the "pain-pleasure-gap (PPG)," which compares the emotional state people are in during a service experience. When customers are dissatisfied about something, Lee maps it to 'pain;' if they are satisfied, it would be mapped to 'pleasure.' Every point in the service journey will have a different emotional measure, some better than others. Excellent service requires a lot of capital, but it isn't necessary to be excellent at all points at all times. Leading brands know this is a significant part of service design, and have this down to a science. The reason, as we shall come to see, is because contrast is necessary in order to *maximize the productivity of finite company resources* and to deliver a memorable customer experience.

## THE SERVICE TRIFECTA™

So, let's be clear: good enough ... isn't! You may have done an okay job in the past, but customers expect more as they consume other experiences every single day. Once consumers discover one-click-anything, they are no longer waiting for it to be invented; they only want to know why you're not offering it. In other words, what got you *here* won't get you *there*.

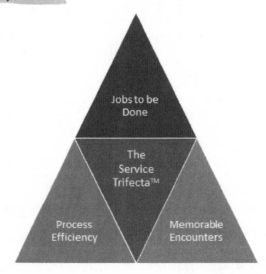

Effective, memorable service delivery takes hard work. The best way for many companies to achieve this involves the use of a comprehensive methodology that considers the goals and objectives that customers, companies, and their employees have in the service-delivery process. It's a methodology that identifies jobs to be done, process efficiency, and the importance of memorable encounters. I call this The Service Trifecta™.

## THREE PILLARS

True to the name, there are three components to The Service Trifecta model, all of which will be explored in greater detail in the following chapters. The first pillar involves figuring out precisely what the customer needs at this moment—what leading academic and business consultant Clayton Christensen would call the "job to be done." As we will see, most companies are awful at this, and it sets the entire service process off on the wrong foot.

Once we've identified what it is that needs to be done, we need an efficient process to do the job. In the second pillar of the model we explore where the cost elements are in service delivery. This is where most companies place their focus, but for all of the wrong reasons: they are fixated on costs, rather than the drivers behind the costs. Because so many companies start—and end—the service process on this single pillar, they miss the other two at their peril. Ironically, because these companies ignore the other pillars, they end up cutting costs—and corners—in all the wrong places. They become so obsessed with cost containment that they end up in a downward spiral, failing to realize they can never cut their way to growth.

19

The third pillar involves the importance of memory: how people involved in the service-delivery process feel about their experience. Iconic companies are iconic largely because of the emotional connection they make with their customers. Everything they do considers the emotional impact each specific step will have on the customer. That's not to say that everything is designed to be a walk on the beach with a pretty girl and a poodle, but there's a keen understanding of how the emotion is tied to the brand. Where is the transition point for customers waiting on line on the spectrum between "There must be something really good waiting for me—just look at the lengths people are willing to go through to get some!" and "I don't care how good it might be, I've got better things to do with my time than stand here"?

After we look at each of these three pillars in detail, we need to see how they all work together during a service encounter. Because every customer and every encounter is unique, the effective-service process considers all three as if their interdependence were being managed with a joystick: rarely in the center, but aware of all three pillars regardless.

## APPLICATIONS

Next, we'll look at some use cases that help to understand The Service Trifecta™ in action: how that joystick is being maneuvered in real time. Where is the emphasis, why is it there, and what is it driving? How do we simplify the process, minimize the cost, and satisfy the customer in a way they will remember and share with their friends?

Then we consider various methods of adopting The Service Trifecta™ in your organization. How will you socialize the importance of these concepts, and manage change with key stakeholders who may not share your enthusiasm?

Finally, we'll lay out the building blocks of a plan that will help you implement the concepts of The Service Trifecta™ in your company. How can you get beyond wishing and hoping to a point where real action is taking place? How can you see real results in a relatively short period of time?

Along the way, I'll share anecdotes and observations from work I've performed with clients over the past three decades. These examples offer excellent insight into the challenges companies face in providing service to their customers, and the even larger challenge of attempting change on a massive scale. We are all creatures of habit and can find many ways to justify the world we live in. Until the pain of remaining the same is greater than the pain that comes from change, we just keep on doing the same old thing.

The purpose of this book is to give you the concepts and a plan to achieve greatness. Your mission, should you decide to accept it, starts by turning the page.

# CHAPTER 2:
# WHAT JOB WERE YOU HIRED TO DO?

*"It's not that they can't see the solution.*

*They can't see the problem."*

**-G.K. Chesterton**

IN THE FIRST part of The Service Trifecta™ we establish why most companies are so bad at figuring out what they should really be doing. We'll then look at two things you need to consider to avoid the same traps: the job to be done, and what caused the interaction with the customer.

## BREAKTHROUGH MOMENTS

After years of working in and observing others in customer service I had an epiphany, a single moment of clarity that summarized for me the frustration of every consumer: *most companies are downright awful at figuring out the real reason why customers need service.* Take a moment to let that sink in. Think about the last time (or three) when you had a reason

23

to contact customer service, then ask yourself: *Did they really understand why I called?* It turns out that your "problem" and my "solution" are often two different things.

Allow me to illustrate. One task I performed while conducting an operational assessment at an automotive finance company involved service-performance observations of their customer-care representatives. Their primary purpose is to speak with customers who financed vehicles the company's dealers sold or leased to customers and resolve any issues related to the loan. Here's what one conversation sounded like between the customer and the agent (although several others that I've observed in other places have been eerily similar):

Agent: Hello, my name is Julie. How can I help you today?

Customer: Hi Julie. I leased a new car from you several months ago. When I signed up for the lease, the salesman told me you would be making an automatic payment against my checking account every month in the amount of $400. I was just balancing my checking account today and discovered that the last payment deducted from my account for this lease was in the amount of $410. I checked the last three months and found that you have been debiting my account for $410 every month. I'm calling to find out why and where that extra $10 per month has been going?

Agent: I'll be happy to look into that for you!

[Much typing by the agent]

24

Agent: Well, I've managed to pull up your account, and it looks fine to me!

Customer (somewhat annoyed): Yes, I know, but what about that extra $10?

[More typing by the agent]

Agent: Well ma'am, I'm looking at your account and there isn't a payment due at this time.

Customer (somewhat more annoyed): Oh, I know that, but that wasn't my question. Where is that extra $10 going?

[More typing by the agent]

Agent: There doesn't appear to be a problem with your account. Is there anything else I can do for you?

Customer (very annoyed): Yes, transfer me to your manager!

After listening to several calls much like this, I went down the hall to the quality-monitoring department. I asked the quality team to gather for a calibration session (a standardized scoring process used by quality teams to ensure all evaluators are using similar measurements). They all got a blank evaluation form and listened to the call I had observed with agent Julie. When the review ended, I asked for their assessment. Here's what they told me, based on the questions on the form:

- Greeted the caller: yes. 20 points!
- Introduced herself by name: yes. 20 points!
- Asked what the problem was: yes. 20 points!
- Used the customer's name during the call: yes. 20 points!
- Asked if there were any other questions that could be answered: yes. 20 points!
- Add it all up, and we'd give Julie a perfect score of 100 points. Which is not surprising, because she's one of our very best agents!

Astounded, I had to ask: But what about the fact that the call got transferred to a manager? "Well, some customers just like to complain! It happens," they replied. "But Julie did a great job, she knows how to handle the tough ones!"

So not only did Julie fail at correctly identifying the customer's problem, the quality-monitoring department failed to put Julie and all of her colleagues on the right path because they focused on all the wrong things! How is it possible that everyone could speak the same language, use common terms, and arrive at vastly different conclusions? It's as if customer service is systemically designed to perform a "drunkard's search" by looking in the easiest place for answers instead of the place that might yield results.

## PROBLEM COMPREHENSION

In *The Chocolate Conversation*, Rose Fass mentions attending a party where everyone was asked to "Bring Your Own Chocolate." She made a decadent cake with a high percentage of cacao and was sure she would impress everyone there. But she didn't. One man at the party said he preferred a Snickers candy bar to get his "chocolate fix." Both are indeed chocolate—but clearly of a different standard! In a similar vein, companies and customers frequently have "Chocolate Conversations." Customers are pretty good at knowing when they have a problem and describing the symptoms, but what companies are really good at doing is training their employees to apologize, offer a discount, or waive fees. The two parties are having the same conversation, but companies fail to search for and identify the underlying issues that drove the service failure ... so it remains a mystery.

In grade school we all went through some form of reading-comprehension exercise where the teacher read a story and we had to interpret what it meant. If we apply that same concept to customer service, we land on an exercise that is critical to every encounter: **problem comprehension**. Most companies are lousy at this, and we need to understand why: Why doesn't this drive you as crazy as it does your customer? If the key stakeholders are incurious about the root causes of service issues, they will remain unknown—and they will also be unresolved!

## JOBS TO BE DONE

The misalignment portrayed above occurs because there is a disconnect between what most companies think they're offering and what people are really seeking. As Theodore Levitt put it, "People don't want to buy a quarter-inch drill. They want a quarter-inch hole!" We might go a step further because nobody really wants a hole either; what they want is to hang something, so they need a hole, which takes a drill. Clayton Christensen explores this in the book *Competing Against Luck*. The central idea behind what has become known as Christensen's

"Jobs to Be Done Theory" is that "your customers are not buying your products, they are hiring them to get a job done." Christensen defines a job as "the progress that a person is trying to make in a particular circumstance."

What specifically do people want from *you*? What job are they hiring you to do, and how would you know? There are two ways to find out:

1.  **Internally**, based on what we know about this customer and this situation. This is done by examining contextual information, anticipating possible outcomes, then leading the customer to the right solution. What do we know about past interactions with this customer? What do we know about similar interactions with other customers? What happened before the customer called? What information has the customer provided during authentication and self-service? Did we do anything that might cause the customer to reach out to us, like mail them a letter or send them an offer?

    For example, banks know when they decline a transaction a customer attempts to make with a credit card. At the instant when the merchant submits a purchase request, the bank can text the customer: "A transaction for your credit card is about to be declined. Click this link to speak to a representative." If both parties know what this is about, they can very quickly resolve the issue. At the same time, if this is a fraudulent transaction, the customer will immediately know what's going on and can work with the bank to prevent fraud.

2.  **Externally**, we can ask the customer: In your own words, what can I do right now to help you? That part is easy. The hard part

is to overcome human filtering and bias in order to objectively process the response. We know that humans do this to weed out those parts of a conversation they think are a distraction. Customer-service agents do it to quickly get to a place where they can align the customer's story to their own understanding of why things are the way they are. Sometimes this can be an efficient technique to filter the noise that is present in all conversations, but in many customer-service situations, it can be dangerous. Leading brands know this and actively train and test their staff on a regular basis on techniques to mitigate bias.

Once we have identified the job to be done, we need to find out why this event happened in the first place. Regardless of the approach, there is one underlying question that should always be considered: What caused this?

## 5 WHYS

The best technique for doing this and really getting at the true cause of a defect or problem is known as "5 Whys" technique, originally developed by Sakichi Toyoda. Not all problems will have a single root cause, so this may need to be repeated with each element discovered in the interrogation process.

For example, "This bill doesn't seem right."

1. *Why?* The total is not what I was expecting.
2. *Why?* The amount you charged me is not what the contract stated.
3. *Why?* It's overcharging me $10.

4. **Why?** The ACH (automated clearing house) electronic-funds-transfer system took more than it was supposed to from my checking account.
5. **Why?** An error was made when the auto-draft amount was entered into the finance platform.

The key is to ask questions without assumptions, distinguish causes from symptoms, and avoid jumping to conclusions in order to find the process that is broken or doesn't exist.

---

## Take the Test: What job were you hired to do?

Before we can solve a problem, we first have to know what the problem is—the job you were hired to do. Here are some questions that will help you assess the problem-comprehension abilities of your employees.

Score your answers as follows:

- Never = 0
- Sometimes = 1
- Always = 2

| Question | Never | Sometimes | Always |
|---|---|---|---|
| 1. We measure the frequency of customer interactions that are transferred or escalated. | | | |
| 2. We investigate at least 10% of transfers/escalations, and 100% for new-hire employees. | | | |
| 3. We listen for key words in customer interactions (voice and text), either with interaction-analytics software or live monitoring, such as "no," "supervisor," "manager," "wrong," "stupid," and so on. | | | |
| 4. We assign a confidence level to reason codes (how problems are classified) used in interaction tracking tools to ensure we know what we are fixing before we take action. | | | |
| 5. We have a procedure to capture the first reported instance of a problem (e.g., an option in self-service for "none of the above" so we will know this is a new issue) that received heightened attention. | | | |
| 6. We restate what we believe is the real root cause of the problem to the customer and ask the customer to confirm by asking, "How confident are you that I understand your problem?" before moving on to find a solution. | | | |
| 7. We measure the frequency of reopened customer issues as an indicator that we did not fully understand the problem before we attempted to solve it. | | | |
| 8. We use gamification tools with our employees to improve their skills at finding the root cause of a problem. | | | |
| 9. Our staff are assessed on their problem-comprehension skills. | | | |
| 10. We consider the entire range of contributors when looking to identify the root cause of service failures, including external companies we rely on as part of our brand promise that are often invisible to the consumer (e.g., suppliers, inventory management, and logistics companies). | | | |

Results: The maximum number of points possible is 20.

- 0–10: You lack the ability to figure out why your department exists.
- 11–15: You're getting it right some of the time, but you still have transfer rates that are too high.
- 15–20: You're doing a pretty good job—and could be doing great with a bit more focus!

---

The right answer to the wrong question is still the wrong answer. Taking the time to figure out the right question—the job to be done—is not easy, but it's a foundational step in customer service.

# Chapter 3:
# How Will You Do
# the Job Efficiently?

*"The shortest distance between two points is a straight line."*

**-Archimedes**

IF YOU CAN'T get interactions down, it won't matter how "right" you are in assisting customers. In the second part of The Service Trifecta™ we explore why most companies take so long to fix what seem like simple problems and how you can avoid the same traps. We do this by considering the role of process efficiency in service delivery.

## Process Efficiency

In the Disney handbook *Be Our Guest*, the importance of properly designing service is clearly explained:

> Think of process as a railroad engine. If the engine does not run properly, it does not matter how friendly the conductor acts or how attractive the passenger cars look,

the train will still not move and the passengers will not pay
their fares. Process is the engine of Quality Service.

One of the most significant milestones most of us will ever experience
is buying a home. The first adventure involves finding something in the
right location, with the right amenities, within your budget. Then you
get the thrill of a lifetime trying to obtain a mortgage for the home, a
process that takes weeks and keeps you on edge the whole time because
you don't know if you'll get the loan or what the rate will be. It works
like this: after you submit a loan application, the loan officer will have
at least a million questions and will want every financial document you
ever possessed (and a few you didn't). Then, just when you think things
have been a little too quiet, the loan officer will call you and ask for
even more documents or maybe a letter explaining something. You'll
eventually get through all of it, only to face a mountain of documents
that need to be read and executed during closing. It's enough to drive a
normal person insane.

I've been through the process many times for new loans, to
refinance existing loans, and for home equity lines of credit. Nearly all
were equivalent to having a root canal. But I found a company quite by
accident that showed me it could be done in a much better way. The
Holy Grail!

One evening I was watching television and saw a commercial for an
online-only mortgage company (no retail locations) that promised three
critical things up-front with one phone call: (1) they would tell you if
they were going to give you a loan, (2) they would lock in the rate, and
(3) they would tell you when the loan would close. All three of these
commitments had been completely out of the question for any bank

I'd dealt with in the past, and I had to find out if it was real! I called the number on the screen, and here's what happened.

The agent greeted me and asked why I was calling. I referenced the commercial I'd just seen on television and asked if the three promises were valid. The agent said he needed to ask me about five questions, then commit to the three promises.

The questions asked were all fairly simple:

1. Who would be on the loan (just me)?
2. Where was the property located and what was the current value of the home?
3. How much would need to be financed?
4. Was I employed, how long had I worked for the company and in this industry, and how much did I earn?
5. What was my current FICO score?

At that point the agent said the mortgage company was able and willing to offer me a loan, quoted me a rate that was substantially lower than my existing mortgage, and said the loan would close in fourteen days. He then asked if I wanted to move forward. Of course, I said yes! He said he would send me an email with an electronic loan application and a list of things they would need (current loan statement, recent tax returns) and asked me to respond within twenty-four hours. I attached everything in one email, got one phone call from them to confirm everything was fine, and arranged a date for closing. Then it got very quiet. For fourteen days. And then the notary showed up, as scheduled, with all of the paperwork ready to go.

In sharing that story with another bank, I learned that they were well aware of how successful this company had become. My previous mortgage had been with this bank, so I knew from experience that a comparative processing time for them had been forty-five days. What I also learned was that the cost for the big bank to underwrite a loan was nearly three thousand dollars, whereas the online mortgage company could do it for less than half the cost. The secret? They were highly focused on doing only and exactly what needed to be done to secure their interest. They asked the right questions up front to predict which prospects would be a good fit and only started the loan process with applicants who had a very high probability of closing. They cut out all wasted effort and performed only what was necessary. It was as if they had found the shortest path between two points and a way to tame the sea of uncertainty.

## Customer Journeys, Service Episodes, and Service Encounters

There are three ways of looking at the relationship companies have with their customers. At the highest level, every customer that belongs to a company has a **lifetime journey** with a beginning, a middle, and an end. Someone might open a checking account at a bank, then sign up for a credit card, then one day take on a mortgage for a home.

Along the way, both parties want or need something from the other. The business wants the customer to buy and consume more (company intent), and the customer will occasionally have issues that need to be addressed by the company (customer intent). These can nearly always be grouped into **service episodes**. The banking customer might attempt to make a purchase using their credit card and have it declined by the merchant, or want to dispute a charge or fee made to their account. These situations are difficult to resolve with a single call to customer service; they frequently require multiple interactions because of the need to research various aspects of the complaint.

Within these service episodes, the company and the customer will have **service encounters** to identify and resolve issues. These involve the use of a wide range of interaction channels that can be as low-tech as regular mail or very hi-tech with artificial intelligence. Most will fall somewhere in the middle by using the telephone, email, or chat or text services.

Start by considering the array of things that could be going on in the service galaxy, who initiated the need for an encounter, and what each participant will expect from the other.

| Company | • Letter<br>• Statement<br>• Offer<br>• Query | • Want<br>• Problem/Issue |
|---|---|---|
| Customer | • Want<br>• Problem/Issue | • Letter<br>• Statement<br>• Offer<br>• Query |
| | Proactive<br>(Initiated By) | Reactive<br>(Responded To) |

Service-episode goals and objectives for both the company and the customer have been plotted in this matrix in two ways: proactive and reactive. The company initiates a service episode when they send something to the customer in the mail, make an outbound call, send a text message, or launch pop-up boxes on the website that position an offer or ask a question. The customer initiates a service episode when they want something or have a problem or issue that needs to be resolved by the company. In corresponding fashion, when one party initiates something, the other is obliged to respond.

## REDUCE THE DISTANCE

Many things happen from the moment the company or the customer identifies something they want or need (a job to be done) until that need has been met. A rock-solid service-delivery process can be measured by finding the shortest distance between the problem and the solution. This includes identifying who the customer is, how they are segmented into groups of customers with similar characteristics, contextual information about them / their journey / this episode, and the purpose of this encounter. Only then can the company identify intent, anticipate future events or outcomes, and find a recommended course of action, not only by starting in the past and working forward, but also by postulating a possible future state and working back to the present.

When a service episode is in play, the company must decide how they want to work through the issue to get to the one right answer as quickly as possible. Customers don't want choices or options; they want only and exactly what they want. The first step involves assembling a list of all of the possible things they *could* do. This is really how customer journey maps ought to be compiled: what are all possible places someone might begin with this issue, where might they end, and what path will they take to get there? After considering each path, the company needs to act on the thing they *should* do, that is, land on the one that will deliver the optimal result for both sides of the equation.

Consider the choices a barista offers to customers at a coffee bar. There could be ten different types of coffee in three sizes with no fewer than half a dozen flavor additives plus cream and sweetener. Yet the typical customer orders the very same thing every time they visit.

The same thing happens in every service episode. When a patient calls the clinic, they don't want to make an appointment, they don't want to know where the clinic is located, they don't want to wade through the staff directory, and they don't want to leave anyone a message. What they want is to speak to their doctor. Nothing more, nothing less.

## EFFECTIVE SERVICE DELIVERY

So, what does an effective service process look like?

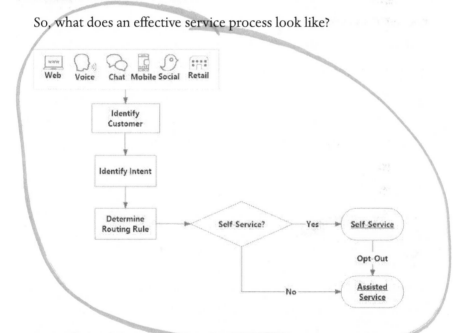

Regardless of the interaction channel of the customer's choice, the first step involves identifying the customer. The official term for this is **authentication** (the process or action of verifying the identity of a user), which should be done as much as necessary and as little as possible. In other words, if it doesn't add value, don't do it. The customer shouldn't have to authenticate just to find out how late you're open. They do need to authenticate in order to personalize the service, however, and in those cases the preferred methods include:

- Online/chat/social: user name and password
- Voice: minimally, the caller ID; for more advanced needs, voice biometrics
- Mobile: app installed on the device

When the customer identity has been established, the next step involves identifying intent. In the service-galaxy grid, we identified **two types of intent: company** and **customer**. Most interactions are driven by one of the elements listed in the grid:

- Clinic wants to alert patients that flu shots are available
- Customer received a statement and doesn't understand a charge
- Customer wants to appeal a denied claim

For company intent, it's critical to deliver the right offer at the right time in order to achieve the right consequence. For customer intent, it's important to understand things the company may have done that could be drivers for the encounter. There can also be situations where intent is present for both parties. For example:

> The customer is remodeling their kitchen. They have met
> with a designer at the home center and know how much
> the remodel will cost. They call the bank to inquire about
> increasing the balance limit on a credit card (**customer
> intent**). In reviewing the request, the bank is aware that

the customer owns their home because they carry the mortgage, have a good FICO score, and have a good payment history on the credit card. But the bank also knows that the credit card is an unsecured loan, has a high interest rate on the balance, and could cause a challenge for the customer later on. So instead of raising the balance limit on the card, the bank suggests a Home Equity Line of Credit (HELOC) to the customer for anything related to the kitchen remodel project (**company intent**). Because the HELOC is secured by the home, it reduces the risk to the bank for extending credit. This meets the customer intent for access to credit, and meets the company intent for securing the bank's interest.

After the intent is known, it's time to make a decision: Where is this type of need best handled? Low-level, redundant tasks can often be fulfilled with self-service, particularly online and with mobile apps. Examples include balance inquiry, mobile deposits, transferring funds, making payments, filing a change of address, submitting claims, checking on the status of work in progress, processing upgrades, and making seat selections.

If the customer is unable to complete the task in self-service or the task is too complex to be handled by automation, it will need to be routed to a live agent with the requisite skills and proficiencies to assist. When the call or chat is delivered to the agent, relevant contextual history should be presented to the agent to help them do their job and make the interaction as efficient as possible.

## Measuring Results

In general, efficiency is a measurable concept, quantitatively determined by the ratio of useful output to total input. Few companies have a deep understanding of efficiency in service delivery. Most simply consider the payroll cost for employees in direct contact with customers, divided by the number of transactions counted. This approach fails to account for the cost of facilities, technology, support, quality assurance, supervision, workforce management, and reporting, not to mention the root cause of the problem.

To arrive at manageable costs, focus on three areas:

- Direct labor of the staff interacting with customers and their supervisors
- Direct operating expenses such as computers, communication equipment, and supplies
- Indirect operating expenses such as facilities, managers, workforce management, reporting and quality monitoring

The goal is to find ways to identify, achieve, and sustain optimal improvements in productivity. These will change over time as the company and its processes mature. What accounts for initial success is different from what's needed to hold on to gains or improve even further. Low-hanging fruit is easy; big gains take a lot more work. Be prepared for the fact that significant early improvements will eventually produce diminishing returns. If you have a deep understanding of these three areas, it will help when you ask for funding for change. It will also tell you where you will be expected to sustain improvement if you want to keep your job and get approval for the next big thing. Be clear; be consistent.

Regardless of the approach, there is one underlying question that should always be considered:

*Based on everything we know at this moment in time, what is the best thing to do?*

---

## TAKE THE TEST: HOW EFFICIENT IS YOUR COMPANY?

Finding the shortest distance between problem and solution is the best way to serve a customer, and it's also the least expensive. Here are some questions that will help you assess the efficiency of your service process.

Score your answers as follows:

- Never = 0
- Sometimes = 1
- Always = 2

| Question | Never | Sometimes | Always |
|---|---|---|---|
| 1. We identify the root cause of problems and fix them in order to minimize waste and rework. | | | |
| 2. We do not ask our customers to repeat information we should already know. | | | |
| 3. We actively solicit input from our customers and employees on ways to improve the service process, and to test the usability of our website and all interaction channels. | | | |
| 4. We know at a granular level what our costs are for service delivery. | | | |

| Question | Never | Sometimes | Always |
|---|---|---|---|
| 5. Our customer-service department is a profit center because we find the owner of the problem and charge them for each interaction we have with the customer. | | | |
| 6. We have a single source of information to minimize confusion. | | | |
| 7. We map all known paths a customer could take when resolving an issue and actively work to guide them in the right direction. | | | |
| 8. We know when our actions are likely to drive customer response and plan accordingly. | | | |
| 9. We leverage contextual information when making task-routing decisions and present the relevant information to the agent. | | | |
| 10. We leverage our technology to find the most appropriate resource to do a job. | | | |

Results: The maximum number of points possible is 20.

- 0–10: Your customer service is abysmal. But you probably already knew that.

- 11–15: You're getting it right some of the time, but your cost to provide service is still too high.

- 15–20: You're doing a pretty good job—and could be doing great with a bit more focus!

---

Using technology to make a good copy of a bad process only allows you to get bad results more quickly. Nail the process first, then look for ways to offload redundant tasks with automation.

# Chapter 4:
# How Can You Create an Effective, Memorable Experience?

*"I've learned that people will forget what you said, people will forget what you did, but people will never forget how you made them feel."*

**-Maya Angelou**

I ONCE WAS offered an opportunity to have a photograph taken of me using the collodion or wet-plate process that dates to the mid-nineteenth century in the early days of photography. I was only vaguely familiar with what that even meant, but it piqued my curiosity so I accepted the offer. The photographer turned out to be Piotr Pietryga, one of the few people keeping this art form alive. I went to the studio thinking it would be the usual "sit here, look this way, smile, thank you" process that every other photographer uses. I could not have been more wrong.

The first thing Piotr did was explain what the wet-plate process was. As he talked, he had me do the work while he explained the steps and chemicals being used. It involved preparing a glass plate with collodion in the darkroom, rotating the plate to be sure it reaches all of the corners, then immersing the plate in silver nitrate for a few minutes. Then the plate is loaded into a frame to protect it from light while moving from the darkroom to the studio, where it can be inserted into the camera.

Then Piotr explained the different types of lenses the camera could use, how they worked, and the reason for having different types. He handed me a lens and had me insert it into the camera. He directed me to sit in the designated spot, a bench in front of a mirror, and then asked me to look at the camera. He said, "What do you think about this camera? What is it saying to you?" I studied this antique contraption for a while and replied, "I think it wants to be my friend." He said, "Show me what you mean!" I stood up and walked to the side of the camera, the place where Piotr would normally be standing if he were going to take the portrait, and I leaned on the camera as if it were an old friend. I could now see myself and the camera in the mirror behind the bench where someone normally would have been posing for a portrait. Piotr handed me the shutter release and gave me a direction: "Press the button, count to three, and let it go."

Finally, he had me take the plate back to the darkroom to develop the image, then fix it in cyanide. We had many laughs about the chemicals, but I had to ask: "If you get a difficult client, do you just add some of this to their tea?"

When I came back later to retrieve the portrait, I was speechless. I'm certainly no model, but what Piotr had captured was unlike anything I'd ever seen before. More importantly, all he did was tell me what to do—in an expert way, mind you. Remember, I did all the work, and therefore was intimately familiar with and involved in the process. That's something that rarely happens. But like that photograph, the entire experience is permanently etched in my memory.

Oh, one more thing. If you look closely at the portrait, you will see Piotr in the background, forever reminding me of an unforgettable moment in his studio.

## THE POWER OF MEMORIES

Anyone who has ever been to Disney World can tell you what they went through to plan for the event and how exciting it was to finally be there! Before the trip, people create what we might call "anticipated memories," followed of course by the memories created from the visit. Those memories are driven by the emotions the experience creates, which are unique to every single person. The very same thing happens when consumers engage with companies. In the third part of The Service Trifecta™, we explore how—and why—companies create memorable experiences.

Before customers reach out to a company, they already have in their minds an idea of what they want, how big a deal it should be, how much it will cost, and how long it should take. That is the "anticipated memory." Then reality sets in. They go through the experience. And there is a moment of truth: What memory will they have after this is done? There are only three possible answers: a **good** memory, a **bad memory**, or worse, **no memory** at all. A good memory is one that will be shared with others, deepens the loyalty, and drives new opportunities. A bad experience may also be shared, may fracture the relationship, but can be repaired if the company has service recovery methods in place. When no memory is created, the customer simply moves on and never returns. Here are a few examples to illustrate.

- One winter a few years ago, I made a short trip to New York to visit a client. On the flight to New York, I exchanged pleasantries with one of the flight attendants, mainly comparing how much time both of us spend on airplanes. The next day, after the meeting with the client was finished, I had to walk through ankle-deep slush to get to a taxi. As I sat in the cab with wet feet on the way to JFK airport, I could see that snow flurries had started up again and I wondered if my flight would be on time.

  When I got to the terminal, I made my way to the gate, checking the monitors along the way. I could see that most flights had been cancelled due to the weather, but mine was still on time. But as luck would have it, just as I got to the gate where my flight was operating, it switched from *on time* to *cancelled* just like all the other flights.

  Because the cancellation was due to weather, the airline had no obligation to provide anything to the passengers. The best they could do for me was to put my name on a stand-by list for a flight that *might* be operating early the next morning. So, like everyone else at JFK that afternoon, I settled in for a very long stay at the airport to wait out the storm.

Eight hours later, it was announced that the weather had improved enough to allow the airport to reopen. A much-delayed flight home would now be operating. I had to wait another two anxious hours to find out if my name had cleared the stand-by list. While I was waiting, the cabin crew turned up to board the flight. I noticed that the flight attendant was the same woman I'd chatted with two days earlier. I said to her, "We really have to stop meeting like this!" and we shared a laugh because she and her crew had been waiting just as long as me and all the others.

I finally got a seat assignment and got on the plane. As I boarded, the flight attendant, now positioned at the aircraft door, congratulated me for clearing the stand-by hurdle and welcomed me on the flight. After I took my middle seat in the back of the plane, I looked up to see the flight attendant headed my way. She had in her hand a flute of champagne, elegantly wrapped in a napkin. She presented it to me and said, "I think you earned this!"

Moral to the story: what had all of the ingredients for a disaster turned out to be a **good memory** of a wonderful experience. The secret: one individual, the flight attendant, took a moment to personalize the situation and create a shared experience with a few kind words and a smile. That has more influence on future business than any product feature or special pricing ever could! The cost to the airline: zero. The reward: my unwavering loyalty.

• Last summer my niece graduated from medical school and hosted a reception at a winery in the state where she lives to celebrate with friends and family. Knowing that the event would extend into the evening past the time when the last flight that would get me home departed, I booked the first flight out the next day and a room at a hotel right at the airport. After the reception and dinner, I returned my rental car and made it to the airport, then called for the hotel shuttle to pick me up. It was close to midnight, but I'd known that would happen and included specific instructions when I made the hotel booking that I'd be arriving very late.

When the shuttle driver picked me up, she asked me if I had a reservation at the hotel, which I confirmed. She then told me that the hotel was completely sold out and they had given the last room to someone else. She would be taking me across the state line to a different hotel several miles away.

Imagine my surprise at learning this news, at this time of night, from the driver of the hotel shuttle! She then asked what time my flight was the next morning, as the replacement hotel was quite some distance from the airport and I'd now need to add an extra half hour of travel time to make my flight. That meant a five a.m. wake-up call.

It's worth noting that this particular hotel chain is one I had regularly used. A few months prior to the event, they changed their booking policy in such a way that if you failed to cancel at least two days in advance, they'd charge you for the room. As I had not cancelled, the room was in effect paid for, so they'd been made whole on the arrangement. That change meant there is no longer a need to overbook a property, because they got paid for every single room.

Moral to the story: what had all of the ingredients for an uneventful stay at the airport hotel turned out to be a **bad memory** of an avoidable experience. The hotel had been paid for my stay, knew I was arriving late, and gave that last room away anyway! They got their money but failed to appreciate the personal impact their greed had on me, the customer. The up-front loss to the hotel: zero. The long-term loss: considerable. Prior to that experience I would have stayed twenty or so nights each year at one of their properties. Since the experience, I have not stayed a single night at any of their properties.

• There are occasions when I'm traveling, hungry, and need to find something to eat. The sign for a nationwide restaurant chain appears and I pull in. The surroundings are somehow familiar, but I couldn't say why. The menu is mostly generic and reasonably priced, but I couldn't name any specific item beyond "two eggs plus your choice of bacon or sausage" from the menu. I also couldn't tell you whether anything I've ever eaten there was good, other than saying I've never gotten sick from their food.

Moral to the story: what has all the ingredients (literally) to satisfy my hunger turns out to create **no memory** at all. Even though this chain spends millions of dollars on advertising, no one ever seeks them out. There's absolutely nothing remarkable about the food, the décor, or the staff. They simply meet a need by providing sustenance. They are remarkable for being unremarkable.

## THE REAL VALUE OF BRANDING

One thing all industry leaders share is a desire for consumers using their offerings to be happy about investing their time and attention. If you could secure someone's attention, what would you do with it? How could you deliver an experience that customers would pay for? How would it help reinforce the message of your brand?

The American Marketing Association informs us that a brand is a "name, term, design, symbol, or any other feature that identifies one seller's good or service as distinct from those of other sellers." One important measure of value comes from the way we perceive the distinctness of a given brand. When customers appreciate a personalized experience, they will choose to spend more time with the company serving it to them because they view it as *time well spent*. In the third part of The Service Trifecta™, we explore how most companies fail to appreciate this value by ignoring the power of memories customers need to have about their brand. Then we look at what your company can do to avoid the same traps.

## EXPERIENCE ECONOMY

The notion of "experience" as it relates to a business offering was explored by B. Joseph Pine II and Jim Gilmore in a 1998 *Harvard Business Review* article titled "Welcome to the Experience Economy," although others before them had made similar observations. The "progression of economic value" they put forth explains that the first level involves extracting commodities; the second level happens when commodities are used to make goods; the third level occurs when those goods are used to deliver a service; and the final level is reached when companies take those services and stage experiences. As the progression happens, the competitive position moves from *undifferentiated* to *differentiated*, and the pricing grows from market level to premium. Pine and Gilmore argue that the orchestrated memorable event (the "experience") itself becomes the product. Their work is the foundation for customer-experience management.

Daniel Kahneman is widely known for his research into behavioral economics, the factors we rely on when making economic decisions. He has written extensively about the difference between what we experience and how we remember what we've done. He gave a TED Talk in 2010 titled "The Riddle of Experience vs. Memory" in which he said, "We actually don't choose between experiences, we choose between memories of experiences. And even when we think about the future, we don't think of our future normally as experiences. We think of our future as anticipated memories."

When we apply this to service encounters, it becomes clear why it matters. Think about the steps a customer takes to resolve an issue. They might go online to do some research on the company's website and maybe chat with an agent. They may call the company, navigate the interactive voice-response system, then speak with an agent. Each step of the encounter will produce varying levels of satisfaction according to how much effort the customer has to put forward to get what they want, and how that aligns to the level of effort they think is reasonable to get the job done. The effort and emotional result can be measured at each point in the process and again when the process is complete by utilizing the **peak-end rule**, a psychological heuristic people use to judge an experience largely based on how they felt at its peak (i.e., its most intense point) and at its end. This is the term Kahneman gives to **remembered utility**. If we map the customer journey through a service process and overlay that with the emotional value felt at the peaks (and valleys) as well as at the exit point, we can form an impression of the memory that service experience will create. This is done by leveraging **pain-pleasure management tools** that consider emotion and loyalty, and **touch-point management tools** that consider the facts of service delivery.

The critical part involves three things: (1) Are the measured values at the peaks (and valleys) within an acceptable range, (2) What emotional state was the customer in when the encounter was complete, and (3) How do both of these measurements align to the brand? For example, if the brand promises customers they will get what they need with low effort (e.g., one-click buying), but in fact it is not a low-effort experience, this will be reflected in high levels of effort and frustration—neither of which support the brand promise.

To be clear, *every encounter should be memorable, but not every encounter needs to be an experience*. The central element in memorable experiences involves the degree to which they are personalized. Customers want only and exactly what they want, only and exactly when they want it.

One way this can be measured is by considering the most precious personal commodity of all: time. *Services are time well saved; experiences are time well spent*. Appropriately used, there is a role for both. The critical task in evaluating service delivery involves understanding the difference and knowing where to focus. Reducing the number of instances a customer has to provide their account number is certainly time well saved; using the information provided (account number) to establish context around the engagement and thus personalize the discussion will ultimately be time well spent. In both instances, time is money—so use it wisely!

## EXPERIENCES SUPPORT THE BRAND

How do industry-leading companies create memorable experiences for their customers? Delivering an effective experience starts with how your company has defined your brand. Does the branding make clear what you do, how you do it, and how this is different from offerings by competitors that seem similar? Companies like Apple ("Think Different"), Google ("organize the world's information"), Amazon ("Earth's biggest selection"), Microsoft ("empower people to do more") and Coca-Cola ("refresh the world") achieved iconic status because consumers have a clear idea what they do and how they do it. Those companies hold teams accountable by asking: Does this add to or take away from our brand promise?

## DESIGNING EXPERIENCES

Every company has a different approach for understanding usability and designing memorable customer experiences, but all require a deep understanding of the customer. Most companies find it helpful to create **user personas**, fictional characters representing the person who would use the brand in a similar way and would be likely to have shared goals and behaviors. You'll also need a base set of use cases that describe the typical mission these personas are on. Taken together, these create the foundation for understanding whom you're dealing with and common elements that will drive episodes and encounters.

Once these personas have been formed, the iterative process begins to identify the unique characteristics of an encounter that will create a memory. Think about the five senses and the powerful emotional connection they have that might influence the memory. Consider how your people, process, and technology design can find ways to capture clues the customer provides and use them in an effective way to create a memorable experience.

For example, a banking customer has misplaced their debit card. Emotionally, what frame of mind is this customer likely to be in? Most likely, they're feeling pretty anxious because they know if that debit card finds its way into the wrong hands, they could be financially wiped out. If the bank ignored the customer's immediate need and saw this customer interaction as an opportunity to cross-sell investment services, they would create dissonance by failing to identify and understand the emotional state of the customer.

There are many ways to experiment with designing and refining service delivery that can create memorable experiences. It starts by deciding on a core principle: Is the offering hidden or exposed to the customer? Either way, the story needs to appeal to all five senses.

- Theme park visitors are on an adventure largely based on fantasy. Places like Disney World and Legoland go to exceptional lengths to ensure that everything there supports the theme. Visitors are not sure how it all happens, it just does.

- Shoppers are on a different kind of adventure, more often based on reality but with a touch of whimsy. Places like IKEA want you to feel at home in the mock-ups they create to resemble the place you live, and they give you the opportunity to experiment with different components to find the ones you like. Build-a-Bear Workshop customers go through an interactive process in which the stuffed animal of their choice is assembled and tailored to their own preferences during their visit to the store. These companies have torn down the wall between operations and the customer experience, taking activities that would usually be hidden and featuring them as part of the journey. Their model centers around the notion that building your own furniture or toy can be as much fun as the toy itself, and people will pay money for the privilege of providing free labor.

## EXPERIENCE CREATION TECHNIQUES

Three techniques that you may find helpful in creating memorable service are **rapid prototyping**, **co-creation**, and **flexible focus**. Although these have been individually used by many, the College of Extraordinary Experiences embraces them as core principles.

- **Co-creation** stems from the notion that it is critical for companies to understand the purpose, meaning, and quality of dialogue from the customer's perspective. To do that, you need a place where everyone involved in the process can contribute. This method is an ideation exercise that brings together customers, agents, management, key stakeholders, and designers in order to jointly produce a mutually valued outcome. It facilitates a blend of ideas with input from direct users and observers, and produces ideas that are more well-rounded. Value comes from personalized, unique experiences for the customer. It also provides an opportunity to learn more about customers, and discover enhanced market-performance drivers for the company that will deliver predictable results. The goal is to find ways that the customer is able to personalize their experience with a company's products or services over a lifetime of use to a level best suited to the job that needs to be done. The personalization aspect is what will create the memory. This is a "Yes, and ..." exercise where participants continue to build upon ideas.

Example: think about how Amazon makes recommendations. Each time a customer visits their website, they go on a journey that hops from one product to the next, sometimes resulting in a sale. Aligning these product-hops along with manufacturer incentives requires input from the buyer, the seller, and the logistics company.

- **Flexible focus** is the ability to examine a memorable experience in a way that is elastic and considers events from the larger story down to the smallest detail by zooming in and out at various points in the journey. Humans selectively eliminate sensory inputs that are unwanted or unnecessary. When assessing variables that might contribute to a memorable experience, look for areas where participants place more emphasis on the areas that are meaningful and important to them. This allows the company to see the experience from different angles or perspectives. Which parts of the experience are strategic, and which are tactical? How do social factors influence behavior? How will this encounter contribute toward resolution of this service episode, and how will this episode affect the long-term journey this customer may be on? Think about the photograph produced by a camera. Many things may be in the frame, but only a select few things may be in focus.

Example: If we're designing an experience for a customer, we might zoom in to think at a very detailed level about the actual experience and the memory we want to create. As we zoom out, we might consider how many people it will take to do this and what tools or facilities they will need. If we zoom out even further, we might consider how much it will cost, how many customers would be a fit, and how it will impact profitability over time.

- **Rapid prototyping** enables companies to pivot by using feedback from fast iterations, which allows designers to quickly mock up and test an idea in order to get to a minimum viable product. As Google Ventures design partner Daniel Burka says: "The ideal prototype should be 'Goldilocks quality.' If the quality is too low, people won't believe the prototype is a real product. If the quality is too high, you'll be working all night, and you won't finish. You need Goldilocks quality. Not too high, not too low, but just right."

Prototypes are only meant to convey an idea, not to be perfect. They ensure you're on the right track before you get so far involved that you can't walk away from an idea. This can be done using storyboards, wireframes, models, or mock-ups of the concept. Then put it in the hands of the customers and agents who will use it and observe what happens. After multiple iterations, the usable elements will surface.

Example: Think about how a company or a school might design procedures for what to do in an emergency. If we only have a few minutes warning, what should people do? Collect in an area? Crawl under their desks? What alarm system gets the most attention? You can try several of these things in only a few minutes to observe how people really react, then quickly weed out ideas that are unworkable to land on ideas worth pursuing.

Regardless of the approach your company takes, the central question you need to consider is this: How will you measure the memory you are creating? Will mentions about your company in social media and hashtags on Twitter be followed by "amazing" or "life-changing," or will it be "awful" and "painful" instead? Will you measure referrals by a something like the popular Net Promoter System (NPS)? Will optimizing the mundane drive loyalty in the form of repeat visitors?

---

## TAKE THE TEST: HOW MEMORABLE IS YOUR SERVICE DELIVERY PROCESS?

Service that creates positive memories is better than service that creates negative memories, or worse yet, no memories at all. Positive memories are critical for minimizing customer churn and leveraging existing customers to help find new customers. Here are some questions that will help you assess memories created by your service process.

Score your answers as follows:

- Never = 0
- Sometimes = 1
- Always = 2

| Question | Never | Sometimes | Always |
| --- | --- | --- | --- |
| 1. We know the memory we want our customers to have when they experience our service. | | | |
| 2. We use a formal methodology, such as an NPS, to measure customer referrals. | | | |
| 3. We actively solicit input from our customers on the memories they have about our service, and we use the verbatims (customer comments) to improve service. | | | |
| 4. We track mentions of our company in social media. | | | |
| 5. Our process enables staff to immediately engage with customers who have had a service failure in order to initiate service recovery. | | | |
| 6. We have a method of quantifying the value of a memory. | | | |
| 7. We actively solicit input from our staff on their observations of service delivery that indicate positive or negative memories. | | | |
| 8. We utilize A/B testing on our service-delivery process to identify discrete elements that impact memorable service. | | | |
| 9. We utilize rapid prototyping, flexible focus, and co-creation when designing customer experiences. | | | |
| 10. We research experiences our customers have in other facets of their lives that influence the expectations they have of the experiences we create. | | | |

Results: The maximum number of points possible is 20.

- 0–10: Your customer service is forgettable. But you probably already forgot that.
- 11–15: You're getting it right some of the time, but inconsistency is keeping you from your goal.
- 15–20: You're doing a pretty good job—and could be doing great with a bit more focus!

---

Good service controls costs; memorable service drives profits.

# Chapter 5:
# How Will You Adopt and Socialize Memorable Customer Service Experiences?

*"It is difficult to get a man to understand something, when his salary depends on his not understanding it."*

**-Upton Sinclair**

MOST CORPORATE TRANSFORMATIONS do not end well, in spite of mountains of research, well-meaning people, and large budgets. It's estimated that about three-quarters of change efforts flop: either they fail to deliver the anticipated benefits or they are abandoned entirely. The one-quarter that survive owe much to executive leadership that believes in and owns the change desired. In this chapter we explore the importance of change management in the adoption of The Service Trifecta™.

## Getting Focused

A few years ago, I had the good fortune to be working with the senior vice president of contact centers at a very large bank on a massive transformation initiative designed to create memorable customer experiences. She had been working with her team for some time on the strategy, process, and people issues. Now they were presenting their case to the technology team to figure out the time and cost needed to enable the scope the business team had agreed upon. No matter how many ways they approached the project, the technology team kept coming back with a response that mapped out a two-year plan for achieving the desired goal. She asked me to step outside with her for a moment, and she shared her frustration with me.

Like many business executives, she knew what she wanted to do, and frankly it was a very good plan. But she was out of her element when it came to the technology. She relied on the experts in that field to guide her, but in this case, they were not providing a response she could live with. She was frustrated and could see that this was a linchpin in her ability to achieve a real, worthwhile business goal. She asked me a simple question: Is this goal achievable, and if so, how long should it take? Do they really need two years? Because if so, the board will never approve funding.

I thought about the situation for a moment and then told her: yes, it's a great goal, it's achievable, and it could be done in six months. She then asked me to walk back into the meeting room filled with technologists and map out the plan on a white board. I drew a simple diagram that showed the immediate layout, the long-term layout, and a migration path to get from the present to the future. The approach made it possible for the business plan to be rolled out in six months, with all technology changes that would be invisible to the customer.

She then asked the room: "Is there any reason this plan would *not* work? If so, speak now." The room was silent. After waiting for a long period of time, she then declared: "Great! Then *this* is your new technology roadmap. I'll be working with the business team to ensure we are aligned to use the platform in six months. Thank you." Believe it or not, it was ready on time and on budget. Several years later, it has withstood the test of time and has proven to be the absolute best path the company could have taken.

What happened in this case that allowed massive transformation to be actioned and sustained? As simple as it sounds, a great deal had to do with having a leader who embraced change. Let's not kid anyone when we're talking about making similar transformations at your company: the cast of characters involved is long, and it includes internal and external resources, partners and vendors. Most of them have spent their entire career creating the world they know. It may not be perfect, but they understand it. And anything you're proposing is risky because it might expose flaws in the status quo that could be traced to them personally.

## THE PROCESS OF CHANGE MANAGEMENT

This is not to suggest that there are undisputed facts that the staff cannot grasp. They may disagree with the goal, see it as incomplete, or feel they lack agency to disagree. And in some cases, they may be right. Choosing the right quest is never easy, but it should be a compelling and uncontested priority. John Kotter of the Harvard Business School created a very succinct list of the stages of change—what it takes to give transformation the best chance of succeeding. Briefly, the plan suggests:

1. **Establish a sense of urgency.** Convince at least 75 percent of your mangers that the status quo is more dangerous than the unknown.

2. **Form a powerful guiding coalition.** Assemble a group with shared commitment and enough power to lead the change effort.

3. **Create a vision.** Develop strategies for realizing the vision.

4. **Communicate the vision.** Use every vehicle available and teach by example.

5. **Empower others to act on the vision.** Remove or alter structures undermining the vision; encourage risk-taking and nontraditional ideas, activities, and actions.

6. **Plan for and create short-term wins.** Define and engineer visible performance improvements.

7. **Consolidate improvements and produce more change.** Use increased credibility from early wins to change systems, structures, and policies undermining the vision.

8. **Institutionalize new approaches.** Articulate connections between new behaviors and corporate success and create leadership development and succession plans consistent with the new approach.

Start by defining how the three critical aspects of The Service Trifecta™ are going to work at your company:

• What experience are you creating for the customer?

- What experience are you creating for the employees?
- Why does this matter to the company? Who has agency and responsibility?

Next, identify the measures of success. This is *not* the same thing as establishing achievement levels and goals—that will happen later. For now, focus on methods of measure. After these steps have been taken, you will be ready to work through the "8-Step Change Model" outlined above by John Kotter.

## IRRESISTIBLE FORCE MEETS IMMOVABLE OBJECTS

Several years ago, I was working with a large integrated managed healthcare company on an initiative to centralize physician appointment scheduling. The business model had been for patients to call their doctor's office whenever they needed an appointment, but patients were complaining of inconsistent experiences with each physician they called.

The new model involved creation of a centralized customer-contact center with a single toll-free number. Patients would contact the center to make appointments with any doctor on staff, and the experiences could be standardized, repeatable, and managed.

Initially, the doctors pushed back. Hard. Each doctor had people on staff (often they were nurses) who understood their schedule, patients, outside activities, and back-up options. Their belief was that this could not be replicated in a centralized, non-personal contact center.

In following a process similar to the one outlined above, it came down to a few simple actions that made all the difference. First, the voice of the customer (patient) had to be revealed in its full glory to the doctors. Simply put, the doctors loved the status quo; the patients hated it. No matter when they called, they ended up in voicemail. That was driving down patient satisfaction.

Next, the business case. Every doctor had a minimum of two people on staff to handle appointments. But what if one went on vacation and the other was at lunch? Who was answering the phone then? Nobody, of course. We then took the number of calls offered to the total set of physicians, subjected them to a simple Erlang calculator (a tool that allows you to calculate the number of staff needed for a given number of calls and to meet a given service level), and discovered that centralizing the function of appointment agents delivered a massive benefit to the organization. The same number of calls could be answered with 80 percent fewer staff, in a consistent manner, for a broader set of uninterrupted hours, guaranteed.

The process really got underway when we solicited volunteers. A few of the new physicians who had no real history or ties to the past agreed to a trial. What they found from the beginning was that the patients had a predictably consistent experience, the appointment book was full, the patients were happy, and their nurses were now free to do their jobs as nurses. After the results were presented to the chief medical officer, the decision was made: this would be the new model. No exceptions. Full stop.

## CHANGE-MANAGEMENT LEVERS

Effective change management poses this question: How will you budget and control time, cost, and scope? We've already established the method for scope, but what about the other two elements?

The next component to be tackled is time. Project management professionals use a **Work Breakdown Structure** (WBS) that organizes the team's work into manageable sections. In essence, it aims to divide work into definable increments. From there, the statement of work can be created to include technical, schedule, cost, and labor reporting. This happens at the beginning of the project and precedes detailed project and task planning.

After the scope and time have been estimated, the final step involves creation of costs. Realistic projects take on holistic assumptions to consider the costs for people (internal and external), facilities, and tools including technology. Challenge participants from the beginning: What have we overlooked that needs to be included in order for this to work?

---

## TAKE THE TEST: IS YOUR ORGANIZATION READY FOR CHANGE?

An effective service-delivery process relies on people, who very often come to the table with experience (usually a good thing) and history (sometimes a good thing) that is not always aligned to the mission. For that, we need a discipline to prepare, equip, and support people if we are to have any hope of sustained success. Here are some questions that will help you assess the change readiness of your organization.

Score your answers as follows:

- Never = 0
- Sometimes = 1
- Always = 2

| Question | Never | Sometimes | Always |
|---|---|---|---|
| 1. We have a culture of open and direct communication. | | | |
| 2. We have a robust work environment. | | | |
| 3. We understand the importance of teamwork and foster an environment of cooperation. | | | |
| 4. We have a process in place to track issues and resolution. | | | |
| 5. We make decisions as quickly as is practical for our business. | | | |
| 6. We keep office politics to a minimum. | | | |
| 7. Our employees openly accept change and work within the process to make change successful. | | | |
| 8. Our employees foster a culture of sharing. | | | |
| 9. Our leadership team is respected by the staff for being open, honest, and trustworthy. | | | |
| 10. We understand the organizational structure of the company but minimize the role of authority. | | | |

Results: The maximum number of points possible is 20.

- 0–10: Your employees are not open to change. This is not going to be easy.

- 11–15: Your employees are probably open to change but need trust and guidance from leaders.

- 15–20: You're doing a pretty good job—and could be doing great with a bit more focus!

The French novelist Victor Hugo once wrote, "He who every morning plans the transaction of the day and follows out that plan, carries a thread that will guide him through the maze of the most busy life. But where no plan is laid, where the disposal of time is

surrendered merely to the chance of incidence, chaos will soon reign."
That's a fancy way of saying "plan your work, and work your plan."
Getting your company's staff to a point where they can reliably deliver
memorable customer experiences will take work—lots of it. The
hardest part involves changing old ways and customs and getting buy-in
for methods and procedures that are nimble and responsive to the needs
of the business. An effective change-management process is essential to
success.

# Chapter 6:
# The Service Trifecta™
# in Action

*"The way to get started is to quit talking and begin doing."*

**-Walt Disney**

WEIGHT MANAGEMENT COMPANY Jenny Craig uses weight-loss success stories that show what their clients looked like before and after participating in their program and includes testimonials from people who have followed the plan and want to share results. This can be helpful for selling hope to others who need inspiration to move forward. One reason this works is that it clearly shows what can be achieved. In this chapter we will see The Service Trifecta™ in action, and to do that, we need to tell a story about the future. The best way to do this is to start at the end and work backward.

## MAKING A NOTICEABLE DIFFERENCE

In previous chapters, we've explored various aspects of The Service Trifecta™ by identifying the root cause of customer needs, building an efficient service-delivery process that looks at the **service encounters** customers have during a **service episode**, and the importance of creating memorable experiences. Now it's time to consider how these concepts, taken together, would look and feel in practice. This is where we need to develop an awareness similar to using a joystick to orchestrate the three pillars of The Service Trifecta™. What will the target condition deliver, what will it take to make it happen, and how would anyone know that things around here have changed? After all, if no one can tell things are different, why do it?

## The Beauty of Low-Friction Service

Like many people, I rely on a large, multinational financial-services company to manage my retirement accounts. Most of what they do is a complete mystery to me (and everyone else), and I have to be in just the right frame of mind to have a conversation about my investments. For many of us, historically, those conversations have happened like this: you first go online to look at your accounts, quickly realize you have no idea what you're looking at, and give the company a call. When your call is answered, you enter an account number if you have it handy (which is never) or your Social Security number, then a password based on your mother's date of birth. Then they play an announcement listing your current portfolio balance and recent activity. Finally, they ask: Did that answer your question? Of course, the answer is predictably "no," so they ask you to select from a long list of options that also have no relationship to your call. Eventually you are routed to some poor agent, so you start at the beginning, tell your whole story, pose your question, and then pray fiercely that the poor agent can make heads or tails out of it and fix your problem.

At the beginning of last year, I called my financial company to inquire about annual contributions to a retirement account they manage for me. When my call was answered, they played an entirely new greeting that went something like this: "We're launching a new feature that will make it easier for you to contact us. We're going to record your voice during this call. Next time you call, you won't have to use your account number or password to authenticate. We'll simply ask you to say, "My voice is my password," and you'll be routed to your financial advisor." Then I was connected to the agent to ask my question. After the call, they sent an email to me that said, "We recorded your voice today and will use it to authenticate you the next time you call. If that wasn't you who called us today, please contact us to let us know so we can secure your account. Otherwise, you're all set!"

I found that interesting. But a month later when I went online to see if my contribution had been made, I saw something I couldn't figure out. I'd completely forgotten about the previous interaction so I did the usual thing: dial the toll-free number. But this time was different. Instead of the usual "enter your account number" routine, I heard: "Say 'My voice is my password.'" I repeated the phrase, and then heard: "It looks like you were just online reviewing your account. Would you like to talk to your financial advisor about that?" Why yes, as a matter of fact, I would! In an instant, my call was transferred directly to an agent who said, "How can I help you?" I didn't need to repeat anything!

Finally, after all these years, a company figured out who I am! They knew where I was in a process and what I'd been doing, and they routed me directly to someone who could help. It's over a year later, and I'm still flabbergasted at how easy, fast, and effective that call was! It was as if my prayers had finally been answered.

## Work Backward

So how did they do it? If they started at the end, they would know that what I was looking for is confirmation that a transaction that was very complex by nature had been completed; that was the job to be done. Working back, they would need to know which agent was working on that transaction. Working back, they would need to know that I'd requested that transaction. And working back, they would have to know who I am. So instead of starting with identifying me, they started with identifying the end result on a map, then looking at all of the possible routes a customer might take to land at that spot. It's a completely different way of looking at service design.

## Voice of the Customer

One way to test the validity of the service-delivery process is to ask customers for feedback. Most surveys produce the right answers, but to all of the wrong questions. They tend to favor "Aren't we wonderful?" questions rather than those that ask "Did we actually do something meaningful for you?" It's like asking your child "Are you hungry?" versus "Do you want a peanut butter sandwich?" The first one may or may not get a response, while the other is immediately actionable. You also don't need fifteen questions on a survey to figure out what you really need to know; aim for three really good questions. Consider asking things like this:

- Are we relevant? Do we understand your need? Was our offer or action something you find interesting and compelling?
- Do you trust us? Do you believe we can solve this problem for you?

- Do we waste your time? Are we asking you questions we should know the answer to? Could this have been done better, faster, easier?

Most executives will have a heart attack on that last question because they already know the answer. But that alone should be a red flag: If you know your service is mediocre, how can you justify ignoring opportunities to make it better?

Let's look at some examples of how companies could employ The Service Trifecta™ to deliver memorable experiences to their customers. As we do, keep these thoughts in your mind:

1.  How does this impact my business?
2.  How does my business impact the numbers shown in these reports?
3.  What area should I focus on to increase a critical score by which we are measured?
4.  Where should I invest my budget?
5.  How can this help me grow the business?

## USE CASES

The three ways of looking at a relationship between a company and a customer—the lifetime journey, service episodes, and service encounters—were outlined In Chapter 4. To see how The Service Trifecta™ works, let's consider how it would apply for a need that most people have: property and casualty insurance. Over a lifetime, a consumer might need coverage for an automobile, an apartment, and eventually a home. The lifetime journey would look like this.

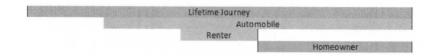

If the goal of the insurance company is to have customers purchase all of their insurance needs in one place, they have to consider this lifetime journey so that they can see the total set of things the customer may use. Then, they start at the end and work backward. They know that more people own cars than own homes, so that's the logical place the customer will start their journey. But they also know they want to sell homeowner's insurance to that same customer. What will they need to do to sell homeowner's insurance to customers with an auto policy? How will they need to manage **service episodes** within each type of policy to earn the right to sell more products to the customer? How will they need to manage **service encounters** within **service episodes** to continue selling that same product to that same customer? In every case the answer is the same: start at the end and work backward.

For each product (automobile, rental, home) there will be a series of service episodes, beginning with the initial encounter to make a purchase, then to renew a policy, and occasionally to file claims. We can break this down into use cases that show the service episodes customers have during their **lifetime journey**.

# INSURANCE USE CASE 1: NEW CUSTOMER

| Job to be done | Provide a quote for insurance, acquire customer, bind policy. |
|---|---|
| How it was solved | Prospect visits the insurance company website, utilizes the quote tool to produce an estimate for auto insurance. A proactive chat window appears with an offer: "We might be able to find an even better price for you. Would you like to chat with an agent to find out more?" The customer engages with the online chat agent and provides more detailed information, resulting in a more attractive rate. The agent asks if the prospect would like to move forward with this rate, and the customer agrees. The agent suggests that the conversation might be easier if they switched to voice, and asks for permission to call the customer. The customer accepts, and the agent places the call. |
| | The agent opens by telling the customer that one of the primary goals the company has for their customers is to make it easy to get service when it's needed. One way that happens is by using voice biometrics on phone conversations to simplify authentication and to ensure security on the account. The agent references the fact that the call is being recorded now, so nothing further is needed from the customer. |
| | The agent confirms all the details the customer entered into the quote tool to be sure they are accurate, including the address where the car will be garaged. The caller indicates she has just finished college and is living with her parents. The agent accepts a payment, binds an automobile policy for the new customer, and completes the on-boarding process. |
| | The agent mentions to the new customer that there are three things worth noting: |
| | 1. They offer customers a **mobile app** where account and policy information can be found. ID cards and proof of coverage are immediately available and can be stored in a mobile wallet so that they are always at the customer's fingertips when needed. The app can also be used to make payments and has a wizard that can assist if there is ever a need to file a claim.<br>2. The company offers a discount to customers who automatically renew their coverage. Two weeks prior to the time when the policy will expire, the company will notify the customer of the rate for the next coverage period. If they accept, coverage remains in effect and the **renewal discount** is applied.<br>3. If the customer has future insurance needs such as a renter's policy, they offer a **multi-product discount** to existing customers. |
| | The day after the policy is issued, a survey is sent to the customer asking: |
| | 1. Did we offer you something relevant to your needs?<br>2. Did the agent treat you with respect?<br>3. Did we waste your time? |

| Job to be done | Provide a quote for insurance, acquire customer, bind policy. |
|---|---|
| Memory created | We're easy to do business with! We have exactly what you need at a great price. We also have more if and when you're ready. |
| Key performance indicators | • Conversion rate <br> • New Customers—volume and value <br> • Lost Prospects—volume, value, and reasons <br> • Revenue and profitability by customer group, and impact on pricing <br> • Referrals by customer group <br> • Effort per conversion |

## INSURANCE USE CASE 2: CLAIM

| Job to be done | Repair windshield |
|---|---|
| How it was solved | The **service episode** happened when the customer was driving on the freeway and suffered a cracked windshield caused by a rock sent airborne by a truck the driver was following. When the event happened, the driver pulled over to investigate the damage. Apart from the cracked windshield, everything else seemed okay. <br><br> The driver remembers that the agent who originally issued the policy informed them of the ability to process a claim from within the mobile app. She opens the app on her mobile phone and launches the claim wizard. The wizard has an option for "windshield damage" that walks her through what she needs to do. She takes a photo of the damage and uploads it through the app. This creates a time and date stamp for when the event happened. The app is also able to use location-based services to determine where the car was when the damage occurred. The app then routes the information to a claims processor for review. <br><br> An hour later, the customer receives a call from the claims processor. He asks the customer when it would be convenient for her to have the damage repaired. She indicates that the next morning would be fine. He confirms the location and time and sends a text message to her mobile phone with an appointment reminder. The text includes a link to reschedule if the customer cannot be available for the appointment. <br><br> One hour before the appointment, the technician scheduled to repair the damage sends the customer a text to advise her he's on the way and confirm she's available as scheduled. She responds yes to the text. The technician shows up as scheduled and replaces the windshield in her car. <br><br> When the technician is done, he cleans all the windows in her car and gives her a kit to clean the windows and a copy of the warranty on the new windshield. She asks what she needs to do to pay for the service, and he informs her that no further action is required on her part; it's all included with the policy. |

| Job to be done | Repair windshield |
|---|---|
| How it was solved | After the claim is processed, a survey is sent to the customer asking:<br><br>1. Did we fix the windshield to your satisfaction?<br>2. Did we waste your time?<br>3. Do you trust us to do the right thing for you?<br><br>The technician calls her one week later to be sure she is satisfied with the windshield repair and there is no evidence of leaks. |
| Memory created | We know things happen. When they do, we'll get you back where you were before the problem occurred in the most seamless way possible. |
| Key performance indicators | • Jobs to be done<br>• Mean time to resolution<br>• Customer effort<br>• Ratio of self-service to assisted service<br>• Customer journey and value |

## INSURANCE USE CASE 3: RENEWAL

| Job to be done | Renew policy |
|---|---|
| How it was solved | The automobile policy has an effective period of six months. Two weeks before the auto policy is set to expire, the insurance company places an outbound call to the customer. The agent greets the customer by name, references the claim for the windshield damage, and asks the customer if she was happy with the service she received from the company.<br><br>The customer replies that she was quite happy and somewhat surprised that things were so easy. The agent tells her that was their goal! The agent goes on the remind the customer that the current policy is set to expire in two weeks and asks if she would like to have it renewed to prevent any lapse in coverage. The customer quite happily says yes. The agent thanks her for the opportunity and reminds her that if her needs changes, they're always ready to help. |
| Memory created | We're looking out for you, so don't worry. We want to be sure you're happy with the service and make it as easy as possible to continue doing business with us. |
| Key performance indicators | • Lost customers—volume and value with reasons<br>• Renewals with reasons |

# Insurance Use Case 4: Renter's Insurance Policy

| | |
|---|---|
| Job to be done | Provide a quote for rental policy, bind policy, build lifetime portfolio. |
| How it was solved | The customer signs a lease on an apartment and the landlord suggests she obtain a rental policy to protect the contents. She remembers the offer made by the agent when she purchased her auto insurance and places a call to the insurance company. |
| | The agent greets her by name and asks how things are with the auto insurance policy and if any problem had come up with the windshield replacement. The customer replies that things are fine and there have been no further incidents after the windshield incident. The agent then asks, "How can I help you today?" |
| | The customer says she is moving to a new apartment and needs to get a renter's policy to cover the contents. The agent asks a few questions about the address and move-in date and prepares a quote. |
| | During the process the agent mentions that she will automatically update the automobile policy with the new address and check to see if there will be any change in rates due to the new location where the vehicle will be stored. Because the vehicle will be in a secure garage, there will be no change in the rate. She calculates the cost for the renter's policy and mentions that the customer is eligible for a multi-product discount. |
| | The agent then asks if the customer would like to purchase the new renter's policy, and the customer says yes. The agent reminds the customer that if she needs any help with the rental policy, the mobile app works for that as well. |
| | The day after the policy is issued, a survey is sent to the customer asking:<br>1.    Did we offer you something relevant to your needs?<br>2.    Did the agent treat you with respect?<br>3.    Did we waste your time? |
| Memory created | We remember you. We appreciate the fact that you trust us and want to do more business with us. We will give you a fair deal and make the entire process as easy as possible for something you'd really rather not deal with but need for peace of mind. |
| Key performance indicators | • New customers—volume and value<br>• Lost prospects—volume, value, and reasons<br>• Referrals by customer group<br>• Revenue and profitability by customer group and impact on pricing<br>• Customer journey and value |

# INSURANCE USE CASE 5: HOMEOWNER'S INSURANCE POLICY

| | |
|---|---|
| Job to be done | Provide a quote for insurance, bind policy, build lifetime portfolio. |
| How it was solved | The customer has been renting an apartment for a year and decides to buy a home. The real estate agent informs her that she will need to obtain a homeowner's policy in order to complete the purchase. |
| | The customer goes online to her insurance company's website to explore options for homeowner's insurance. She uses the quote tool to produce an estimate but isn't sure how to provide that information to the realtor and loan officer processing the mortgage on the new home. |
| | She decides to call the insurance company. Because she's an existing customer, she's asked to say her vocal password. The system immediately recognizes her and asks if she's calling about the homeowner's insurance policy she was researching a few minutes earlier online. She says yes and the call is routed to an agent along with the quote produced online. |
| | The agent confirms the details about the home, including address and coverage amounts. From that, the agent is able to prepare a quote and offers to send it to the realtor and loan officer. The agent reminds the customer that she is entitled to a multi-product discount that also includes a further discount for continued loyalty. The customer is glad to have this task accomplished and happy with the discounted price for the coverage. The agent asks when the home is scheduled to close escrow and makes a note of that date. |
| | On the day before escrow, the insurance company calls the customer to confirm everything is still on track. They inform her that the policy will be in effect when she takes possession of the home and that her automobile policy will be updated with the new address as well. |
| | The day after the policy is issued, a survey is sent to the customer asking:<br>1. Did we offer you something relevant to your needs?<br>2. Did the agent treat you with respect?<br>3. Did we waste your time?? |
| Memory created | We remember you. We appreciate the fact that you trust us and want to continue doing business with us as your needs grow. We will continue to reward you for longevity and increased business, and to make the entire process as easy as possible for something you'd really rather not deal with but need for peace of mind. |
| Key performance indicators | • New customers—volume and value<br>• Lost customers—volume and value with reasons<br>• Renewals with reasons<br>• Revenue and profitability by customer group (and impact on pricing)<br>• Referrals by customer group |

It's important to point out that the **customer lifetime journey**, **service episodes**, and **service encounters** described here use insurance as the vehicle to tell The Service Trifecta™ story but are in no way particular to that industry. The very same thing can be applied to nearly any company, so don't get hung up on these examples as the only way to make the tools work.

While buying insurance may never approach the experience level a customer might have at Disneyland, it's something we all need. If all goes well, it's mostly riding along in the background. But when a customer needs help with insurance, they want it to happen in an efficient way so that they can get back to whatever they were doing before the problem came up. They also want that service delivered in a way that is personalized to their specific needs and situation. Only and exactly what they want.

# Chapter 7:
# What Next?

*"Think Big, Start Small, Learn Fast."*

**-Chunka Mui**

CUSTOMERS OFTEN FORGET service even when it's good, but they rarely forget service failures. And companies that fail to mature and create favorably memorable experiences for their customers run the risk of being seen as a commodity and thus easily replaced. Some companies never seem to rise above ordinary, and we have to wonder: Why? Do they not see the need? Do they not want to be better or even give it a try? Or is it that they fail to comprehend "ordinary" as a problem, in much the same way they fail to comprehend their customers' needs?

## THE PRICE OF MONOPOLIES

Perhaps some companies believe they own the market so doing anything that recognizes the customer is just unnecessary. Cable television companies practically have the market cornered when it comes to customer service that borders on abusive. Even as satellite providers have taken a significant portion of their business, they refuse to change. One clue seems universal: whenever the customer is required to have a subscription, be prepared for poor service.

## OWNING CHANGE

A large bank company that I've worked with over the years has a matrixed organizational structure (employees have dual reporting relationships - generally to both a functional manager and a product manager). As with most companies in financial services, everyone seems to have the job title of vice president of something or other, but they don't have any authority. The people to look for are "managing directors," as they at least have the power to effect change. The level of managing director is akin to a college training program or musical chairs, where no one holds the job for longer than eighteen to twenty-four months before rotating to the next position. The theory is that this approach gives each candidate a broad exposure to all aspects of the company before being promoted into a more senior management position. The reality is that a managing director has very little experience when they come into a new position and no incentive to make changes of any significance. In fact, their real motivation is to run down the clock and make it to the next position safely. The unintended consequence is that meaningful changes only happen when regulatory oversight forces it, but not in any organic way to provide real service to customers.

Now, let's be honest: reliable, sustainable transformation that positions a company for a long and healthy life is not for the weak of heart. It takes time and a lot of work, requires hard decisions, and will cost money. So, you have a choice: you can either be as ordinary as everyone else and end up marginalized and treated like a commodity.

Or you can adopt The Service Trifecta™ and incorporate experience-design concepts into your service delivery in a way that will allow you to go from mediocre to great.

## THINK BIG

The process for transformation has five workstreams:

1. **Identify who your customers are.** Create personas that describe them. What are their characteristics? What will they be like over a lifetime? How will their needs change over time? How will they reflect on experiences with you in a way that builds on previous success to drive the future? How much are they influenced by friends and family? Are those influences based on cultural, regional, generational, age-related, or career-related factors, or some other variable? How are they likely to build trust?

2. **Identify the jobs to be done.** Is there a way to classify these jobs or to create cohorts of jobs with similar characteristics? How can these be quantified or measured in some way?

3. **Identify the drivers behind the jobs to be done.** Looking at the world from the customer's point of view, how do they know when they have a need or a want? What is now the customer's intent? What caused this in the first place? Who owns the responsibility to fix the root cause of the problem? Who should pay for this? How can the driving factors be identified, and how far in advance? Is there any correlation or causality between jobs that would allow you to predict

when one will lead to another? Is this something that can be predicted, or is it more sudden?

4. **Identify the company's intent with typical service encounters.** What do you want to get out of this? What is your intent? How might this lead to the next opportunity? Are you able to identify new offers and competitive threats? What would it take to serve up the next opportunity at exactly the right moment?

5. **How will you know whether things are working?** What are the meaningful key performance indicators for The Service Trifecta™? How nimble is your organization to react when indicators are going in the wrong direction?

Initially these workstreams will happen in sequence, but as they gain traction they will progress in a parallel fashion.

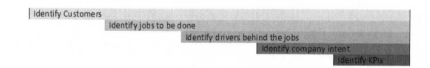

Ultimately, it's not a goal, it's a process. Every single one of these workstreams, once initiated, will take on a life of its own. For example:

- The customer base that exists now will change. Who are the new customers you plan to target? How are their characteristics different? How are the needs of Gen Z customers different from the needs of Millennials, Gen X, or Baby Boomers?

- Will jobs to be done change as the customer base changes? Will new jobs be created? How will you know when existing jobs are no longer in play?

- Will process improvements influence drivers? Will external sources influence drivers?

- What will be the impact on service encounters as the range of company offerings changes over time? How will this impact time to market (the length of time it takes from a product or service being conceived until its being available for sale)?

- As more data becomes available, how is it being used to change service delivery and create memorable experiences for customers? Are existing measures capable of telling the story, or will new measures be necessary? What does an effective service-recovery program look like?

A good way to ensure these efforts are embraced and actioned is to put them in the form of a project charter document. The idea is to gain consensus from key stakeholders on the workstreams that have been identified and agreed upon, as a sign of commitment necessary to influence change. At a high level it will be necessary to define scope, time, and cost for this initiative.

Next, begin identifying resources and forming cross-functional project teams. This is where **co-creation** comes to life. In particular, look for participants who have expertise or bring a perspective that is necessary for success. Don't forget to think about how you will involve customers in the thinking and design of service delivery, and the ways you might create memorable experiences. Pay particular attention to personalities who are not afraid of change but rather see change as an exciting path to the future unencumbered by rules and regulations. Be inclusive, open to ideas, and accepting of constructive criticism.

## Start Small

Now it's time to develop a testable hypothesis and set some key milestones that are intentionally aggressive. It's not necessary to "boil the ocean" or identify all known variables before getting started. We're not aiming for perfect out of the gate. If the project team is made up of smart, nimble people, they should be able to quickly establish many known elements from the outset. At the same time, an effective process allows for the fact that additional material will be added, assumptions will be tested to ensure they are valid, and the design largely prevents clinging to disproven assumptions.

A real asset at this stage is the use of **co-creation**, **rapid prototyping**, and **flexible focus** to run trials and test ideas in order to get to a minimum viable product. One large bank I worked with wanted to reinvent their loan underwriting process but knew they had a legacy to overcome that dated back to the nineteenth century. The resistance to change was practically systemic and had been seen as an insurmountable obstacle in the past. We discussed several options but landed on this one:

1.  Create a pilot built around the principles of The Service Trifecta™.

    a.  Use **co-creation** to work with customers and staff to map out the most efficient method possible to underwrite a loan. Focus on a specific geographic area where many of the data points are already known.

   b.  Use **flexible focus** techniques to zoom in and out on various stages of the process and from different perspectives (customer, agent, company), then ensure alignment.

   c.  Conduct a premortem to identify potential bottlenecks and points of failure, and create a plan to manage them. Think about what could go wrong and be prepared.

2. Trial the pilot for ninety days to see if the assumptions were correct, review findings, and adjust as necessary using **rapid prototyping** techniques.

3. Present an option to the board of directors, based on the success of the pilot, that this is how the loan underwriting process should be done. To implement the new process, either:

   a.  Direct the organization's existing loan-underwriting arm to change and utilize the new methodology created by the pilot, or

   b.  Grow the pilot and shut down the old process.

## LEARN FAST

The idea behind learning fast is to keep an open mind about what you are pursuing. Avoid the temptation to rely on instinct and instead be scientific in your approach. Don't get hung up on subjective emotional attachments that can lead to failure. When **rapid prototyping** is done correctly, it can be a huge asset in the innovation process because tests are designed to produce a result that either works or doesn't. If it does, terrific; if it doesn't, set it aside and move on. Be brutal in filtering out distractions, but stay focused on the end game.

## But Start!

All writers know that you can write until the end of time but eventually you have to publish. There will never be a perfect time; the material will never be fully complete; you will never have all your ideas carved in stone. But if large-scale change is ever going to see the light of day, you have to take a chance. This is where the process of setting aggressive milestones will pay off.

Iconic companies know this well. For example, Steve Jobs, famous for imposing what seemed like unrealistic deadlines on his staff, gave the original iPhone engineers just two weeks to come up with a "software vision" for the company. He threatened to hand the work over to another group inside Apple if they failed. That might sound pretty harsh, but the results are hard to argue with.

## Final Thoughts

The concepts presented here for The Service Trifecta™ are meant to provide the framework for creating effective, memorable customer experiences. No two companies are alike, no two situations are alike, and there is no set of best practices you should be following. If you fundamentally agree with the concepts presented here, then view them as best principles for service delivery and consider how they might apply in your world. Regardless of how you get there, deliver only and exactly what the customer wants, only and exactly when they want it.

I've given you the concepts to get the process started. Now, it's up to you: you have to paint or get off the ladder.

> *In any moment of decision, the best thing you can do is the right*
> *thing, the next best thing is the wrong thing, and the worst thing*
> *you can do is nothing.*

**-Theodore Roosevelt**

# About the Author

**Mark Stanley is** a customer experience designer for Genesys (www. genesys.com). He has worked in and for a variety of customer-service-related companies. During a span of twenty years in the airline industry, he transitioned to the contact center to develop skills around the technology used to connect customers to service staff, as well as the supporting systems used for things like workforce management. He then moved into business consulting and project management, with a focus on the relationship and interdependence between business goals, contact-center operations, and technology.

His areas of expertise include:

- Strategies that deliver an effective customer experience and support the company's brand.
- "Needs analyses" and customer-experience audits based on business challenges within specific industries.
- Implementation of integrated solutions that manage the customer experience.
- Designing effective systems that reduce costs, increase revenue, and control headcount.

Prior to joining Genesys, Mark held several call-center operations and sales-management positions with Crestview Consulting Group, Wolfe & Associates, ERS (a third-party healthcare services provider), Lufthansa German Airlines, and Korean Air. He holds a bachelor of arts degree in history from Loyola Marymount University, is a Certified Experience Economy Expert, a graduate of the College of Extraordinary Experiences, a COPC Implementation Leader, and a Project Management Professional (PMP)